Life Without Limits

A Guidebook to Turning
Your Dreams into Reality

About Marjorie Brody, MA, CSP, CMC

Marjorie Brody is founder and fearless leader of Brody Communications Ltd. in Jenkintown, PA, where she helps individuals and corporations achieve their potential by strengthening their professionalism, persuasiveness and presence. She has helped thousands of people break through the invisible walls of poor communication and career development. Marjorie has presented to more than 1,000 audiences, and is the author of 16 books, including *Help! Was That a Career Limiting Move?* and *Speaking is an Audience-Centered Sport.* She has appeared on CNBC several times, Fox-TV, Oxygen Network, and has been quoted in *The Wall Street Journal, Washington Post, USA Today, People, Glamour, BusinessWeek, Fortune* and many more national publications.

Life Without Limits

A Guidebook to Turning Your Dreams into Reality

by Marjorie Brody, MA, CSP, CMC

Dedicated to all of those who have helped me live my dreams.

Life Without Limits: *A Guidebook to Turning Your Dreams into Reality*

Project Editor & Design: Laura M. Kremp

ISBN: 1-931148-10-4

Table of Contents

Introduction

A Road Map to Making Your Dreams a Reality

"I learned this, at least, by my experiment: That if one advances confidently in the direction of his dreams, and endeavors to live the life which he has imagined, he will meet with a success unexpected in common hours. He will put some things behind, will pass an invisible boundary; new, universal, and more liberal laws will begin to establish themselves around and within him; or the old laws be expanded, and interpreted in his favor in a more liberal sense, and he will live with the license of a higher order of beings. In proportion as he simplifies his life, the laws of the universe will appear less complex, and solitude will not be solitude, nor poverty poverty, nor weakness weakness. If you have built castles in the air, your work need not be lost; that is where they should be. Now put the foundations under them."

-- Henry David Thoreau, *Walden*

"Never, ever stop dreaming! Some dreams will prove elusive, and some will prove disappointing. Some may seem misguided, and need to be revised, revamped, revisited. But, it is our ability to dream of new and better worlds that makes us human. Our dreams empower us! Our leaders and heroes have always been pulled by their visions, their dreams of possibilities that lie around the corner, just out of sight, but not out of reach. Dream big dreams."

-- Philip Humbert

Have you ever noticed how some people are able to go after what they want ... and get it? They seem to be unstoppable.

Many people overcome seemingly insurmountable odds. Yet, others get stuck from their own inertia. They get distracted, they get discouraged, and they give up. Many never even start.

Too many people fail because they wait for things to happen, rather than take an active role in making them happen. Sometimes the enormity of the idea (call it a dream, call it a goal) is overwhelming.

In my role as Executive Coach, I frequently ask clients, "What would you do if you didn't worry about failing?" I hear, "I would love to ... but I guess it is only a dream." They give up before even exploring the possibilities. I have always believed what Henry Ford said, "If you think you can or you think you can't, you are probably right."

My goal for this guidebook is to help you realize that almost anything is possible if you are willing to commit to it, break it down into manageable pieces and, finally, do whatever it takes to make it happen. It's a simple process, but not always easy. That's why so many people fail.

I have used the words "dream" and "goal." They are not the same. A dream is something you think about; often it is the "big picture" or even a bit fuzzy. It can be something outside the realm of possibility, or at least outside the possibility for you. For example, like many people, I have a dream of world peace. Outside of being a good citizen, joining peace groups or supporting politicians that hold the same values, there is little that I can do. Nonetheless, it is a dream.

A goal is something more concrete. Something that you can take small steps and work towards. It can be accomplished. You can have both short-term and long-term goals. You can have small and stretch goals. Whatever goals you have, they should be in the realm of possibility. For example, winning the lottery is a dream. Besides buying tickets, you have no control over it, no matter what you do.

This guidebook is organized to take you through a logical process. It begins with identifying dreams, turning them into goals, finding ways to eliminate obstacles, selecting people and resources to help you and, finally, creating an action plan to make those dreams become reality.

What does it take to make it happen? I believe it requires:

➤ Passion

➤ Persistence

➤ Patience

You'll notice, I didn't mention time, money, etc.

Passion: Is this a burning desire? Are you ready to make sacrifices for it? Can you visualize it?

Persistence: Are you willing to do whatever it takes? Will you keep at it when things don't seem to be going your way?

Patience: Will you wait things out, and take extra time if necessary? Are you a person who doesn't necessarily expect instant results?

If the answer is "YES" to all of these questions, you *CAN* turn your dreams into reality.

This workbook is written to be used in a variety of ways:

1. Individually

2. With a partner (spouse, friend, etc.); the conversations that ensue may surprise you!

3. In groups (an interesting activity to do with colleagues, friends and family)

There are numerous activities to help you along the way. There are also quotes and stories from others who believe in the power of their dreams. Some of the stories are about famous people, others about great athletes. I have also included stories about "regular" people who never gave up.

Here's an example:

Robert walked in to the party, a bottle of wine in hand. He had been friends with the Bradshaws for years and often counted on their holiday party as a much needed diversion.

Still distracted by the strategic plan that he had been working on night and day for the last three weeks, he kissed the hostess, Angela, on the cheek and glanced around the room.

Without warning he spotted her, a woman he had never seen before who was engaged in an animated conversation with two men. He neglected to acknowledge Angela's greeting. Instead, he abruptly interrupted her to say, "Who is she?" as he nodded in the direction of the woman who had already started to make his palms sweat.

"Oh that's Debra," Angela replied. "She's here with her date, Ricardo. They've been together for five years."

"I have to meet her!" Robert insisted. "She is the woman I am going to marry."

With prodding and persuading, Angela agreed to steal Debra away from her date and introduce her to Robert. Before names could be exchanged, Robert had taken Debra in his arms. Shocked she pulled away as Robert smiled and said, "Years from now we are going to laugh about this night when we will tell our children about how we first met."

Debra was only mildly amused. "Who is this crazy man?" she thought. She politely chatted for a few minutes answering the typical questions of where she worked and what she did, but all she really wanted to do was return to the safety of her date.

Robert left that evening more convinced than ever that he had met the woman with whom he would spend the rest of his life. Realizing the touchy position he was putting his friends the Bradshaws in, he decided that he would have to find this woman and speak with her again on his own.

With the thoroughness of his best business plans, he set his objective and strategies. He had become a man with a mission. Debra had mentioned that she worked for Xerox, and so on Monday, he began calling each of the 19 Xerox branches in Manhattan. He came up empty-handed. Robert wasn't about to call it quits. He next called an operator and asked for the names of Xerox subsidiaries. There were 23 of them. He had his list and he made his calls.

Days later Angela picked up the phone to hear Debra on the other end saying, "Who is this guy? Is he crazy? Is he a stalker?" Robert had succeeded in reaching Debra at her office.

The months passed and Robert stayed on task. He called Debra periodically, sent flowers from time to time and always asked when he could see her next. Her predictable "No I can't see you." didn't deter him.

When she did agree to speak with him on the phone, he listened to her describe the long relationship she had been in. He skillfully asked her questions that caused her to reflect on why after five years she had not married the man she had been dating for so long.

Robert's plan also included finding out which commuter trains Debra took each day so that he could arrange for a smattering of serendipitous encounters. Each time he saw or spoke with her, he was more convinced than ever that they were meant to be together.

Several months passed. On two occasions, Debra and Robert saw one another at the home of mutual acquaintances. Debra was slowly beginning to be intrigued by this brazen man, who had so shamelessly embraced her that evening in December. She started to enjoy his sense of humor, his confidence, and she reluctantly gave thought to why her current relationship hadn't gone anywhere.

Further convinced by friends and acquaintances that Robert was a man of integrity and character, she started accepting his calls with a smile. After 16 months, and 23 invitations for a date, she finally accepted, convincing herself that dinner with a friend could do no harm.

That dinner took place 19 years ago. Debra and Robert have just celebrated their 18th wedding anniversary. They smile as they talk about their wedding that took place those many years ago in the living room of the Bradshaws, the very place Robert commented to Angela, "That is the woman I am going to marry!"

This book will break down the process of going from dream to reality. It is a process that has worked for countless people ... a process that can work for you!

"The future belongs to those who believe in the beauty of their dreams."

-- Eleanor Roosevelt

"Hold onto your dreams for they are, in a sense, the stuff of which reality is made. It is through dreams that we maintain the possibility of a better, more meaningful life."

-- Leo Buscaglia

Chapter 1

First Things First ... Write it Down

"*The key to happiness is having dreams. The key to success is making your dreams come true.*"

-- Anonymous

"*The first step to turn your dreams into goals is to write them down.*"

-- Marjorie Brody

As a child, I was always accused of being a "dreamer." My parents would say, "You are only a dreamer, you need to be more practical." I used to wonder, "Can't dreams ultimately end up being practical?" In time, I realized that a dream which stays a dream goes nowhere. It is only when you do something with the dream that things begin to happen. But first, you do need to dream. All great things start with a dream. Contrary to popular belief ... being a dreamer is a good thing.

When is the last time you allowed yourself to dream? To dream big?

The first activity in this workbook is to take some quiet time to think about your dreams. What do you want to do? Where do you want to go? What do you want to have? What do you want to be? It is all doable ... it is just a matter of starting. What is your wish list in each category? Some of these dreams can be way off in the future, others more immediate. Some are hard to do, others more easily done (but not being done at this time for some reason). Brainstorm the first things that come to mind; dream and then push yourself for more.

The dream categories included are:

➤ Career
➤ Financial
➤ Primary Relationship
➤ Other Family
➤ Physical / Wellness
➤ Mental / Spiritual
➤ Leisure
➤ Community Service
➤ Possessions (car, house, artwork, jewelry, etc.)
➤ Add other categories that are important to you

You may not be able to fill in all the categories; that's OK. They are just ways of looking at different parts of your life.

Career

Financial

_____

_____

_____

_____

_____

_____

_____

_____

_____

_____

_____

_____

_____

_____

_____

_____

_____

_____

_____

_____

_____

_____

_____

_____

_____

Primary Relationship

Other Family

Physical / Wellness

Mental / Spiritual

_____

_____

_____

_____

_____

_____

_____

_____

_____

_____

_____

_____

_____

_____

_____

_____

_____

_____

_____

_____

_____

_____

_____

_____

_____

_____

_____

_____

Leisure

_____
_____
_____
_____
_____
_____
_____
_____
_____
_____
_____
_____
_____
_____
_____
_____
_____
_____
_____
_____
_____
_____
_____
_____
_____
_____

Community Service

Possessions (car, house, artwork, jewelry, etc.)

Add your own categories

Did you dream big? Did any of these dreams surprise you?

You may be questioning, "Now what? I have lots of things on paper, but how does that get me closer to doing anything?" Well, the next step will be to create goals out of some of these dreams.

When I started speaking about goal setting, I did a great deal of research to find out what worked for people who set goals and ultimately achieved them. The overwhelming answer was that they **write them down, keep the goals visible, and refer to them regularly**. This was not a surprise, since I have not only been a dreamer, but also a goal setter and list maker. Somehow the writing process adds a level of commitment for oneself, and posting the goals serves as a visual reminder. After all, if you commit to doing something, rather than just thinking about it, it usually will push you forward. Besides, when others hear about or see your goals they may help you achieve them. Going public also helps you own them.

Referring to your goals regularly will remind you to take action. One of my dreams was to be a well-rounded reader (not just business and industry specific). I thought about this for years, but took no steps to make it happen. Then I decided to turn it into a goal. I committed it to writing in my goal journal. I listed each month of the year and left a space to record the name of the book that I read that month. This journal is on my nightstand, and I reference it several times a week. I post my business and professional goals in my office, so I look at them daily. This system keeps me on track. Overkill? Maybe, but it's a system that works for me. What can you do that will keep you on track?

Write down your ideas:

After confirming that writing goals down does make a difference, I did an experiment in my office. I shared the findings with my staff, then suggested (not required) that each person write his or her yearly personal goals and then post them in their office or cubicle. Their lists varied, but some of their goals included:

> Make my sales quota
> Exercise 3-4 times a week, minimally for 15 minutes
> Buy a new sofa
> Spend more time with my son
> Take a trip to Africa
> Reduce my debt

It was interesting to me who actually did the goal setting. When I questioned the group, some admitted that they hadn't thought about setting personal goals, while others said they had them in their head and that was enough. Inevitably, it was the most successful members of my team who actually did it. It was rewarding to see them crossing off one goal at a time. As it paid off, they bought into the concept. Those who did this the first year are still doing it today.

Goal setting is done regularly in many corporations. Of course, those goals are all about the business. Often, people don't take the time or even think about doing this in other areas of their lives.

You have written down your dreams, now it is time to go back and determine which ones you want to become goals. It can happen, but first apply the reality test. Go through each dream and answer the following questions:

> Does it excite me?
> Can I picture it vividly in my mind?
> Am I willing to do it?
> Will I enjoy the challenge of the journey?
> Would its attainment create self-satisfaction?
> Would it be a challenge/risk?
> Is this what I really want?
> Do I believe that I can achieve it?

The purpose of this evaluation is to identify what you think you want and what you really do want. Remember that Passion, Persistence and Patience are all critical factors.

Now that you have evaluated your dreams, go back to your list again and select five dreams that seem to be top priorities. Keep in mind, the purpose of this guidebook is to teach you a process. You can always add to this list. Your dreams can be from the same or different categories.

1. _____

2. _____

3. _____

4. _____

5. _____

Remember the difference between a dream and a goal. A dream is intangible. A goal is concrete. Let's define a goal as a dream with a deadline. It's time to turn your dreams into goals.

Assign a deadline to each dream, turning it into a goal.

Partners
Discuss your dreams and your final goal selection. Were there any surprises? Were there similarities?

Chapter 2

Learning From the Past

"Keep these concepts in mind: You've failed many times, although you don't remember. You fell down the first time you tried to walk. You almost drowned the first time you tried to swim ... Don't worry about failure. My suggestion to each of you: Worry about the chances you miss when you don't even try."

-- Sherman Finesilver

Think of all the times you have been successful in achieving your goals. Think of the times you have been successful in your life. I am sure that your success rate is much higher than your failures, yet people tend to remember and dwell on their mistakes. People are also more apt to point out their weaknesses and not their strengths. I know that I remember every negative comment that was ever put on a speaker evaluation sheet for the past 20 years, yet discount all the accolades.

When was the last time you focused on and celebrated your successes and strengths? This activity will help you do so.

Directions: Read the paragraph below; then answer the three questions on the next few pages.

As humans, we have the amazing capacity, talent and tenacity to go after and fulfill our dreams, overcoming seemingly impossible obstacles. We often discover new strengths and resources within ourselves that we didn't know we had when we face a challenge or choose to pursue a dream. Usually, we have allies who, through their support, help us along the way.

Partners
Read the paragraph and answer the questions together. Discuss what you liked about the person's story? What was a surprise? What inspired you? What did you learn about your partner? Were there common threads?

1. Write about a time when you had a dream that seemed impossible to accomplish; yet you did it. Describe what happened. What were the obstacles you faced and how did you overcome them?

_____

_____

_____

_____

_____

_____

_____

_____

_____

_____

_____

_____

_____

_____

_____

_____

_____

_____

_____

_____

_____

_____

2. What did you do to make this happen? What talents, strengths and resources did you use? Who helped you accomplish this and what did they do? Describe how you felt about this accomplishment and why it was important to you. What did you learn from the experience?

_____

_____

_____

_____

_____

_____

_____

_____

_____

_____

_____

_____

_____

_____

_____

_____

_____

_____

_____

_____

_____

_____

3. How can you most effectively use your own strengths, talents and resources in the future to make your dreams come true? Who can support you, and what can they do to help?

_____

_____

_____

_____

_____

_____

_____

_____

_____

_____

_____

_____

_____

_____

_____

_____

_____

_____

_____

_____

_____

_____

_____

_____

_____

I hope right now you are feeling really good about yourself and you are appreciating your capabilities and resources!

Chapter 3

Obstacles or Excuses? ... You Decide

"*Obstacles don't have to stop you. If you run into a wall, don't turn around and give up. Figure out how to climb it, go through it or work around it.*"

-- Michael Jordan

"*The essential process behind positive thinking is first to set yourself goals and then to imagine them having been achieved. It is not just a question of setting goals, but of seeing in your mind's eye, the goals being fulfilled. The importance of this can be understood in terms of mental set. ... imagining as strongly as possible, the fulfillment of your dreams as already having occurred, sets you positively for events and opportunities that will support your goals.*"

-- Peter Russell

Wouldn't it be nice if, at the snap of a finger or wave of a wand, you could accomplish your dreams?

The reality is, wishing, wanting and whining do not make it happen. Granted, the road to success won't be smooth. You will be faced with twists, curves and many potholes. The question is, will that stop you from reaching your destination?

When I ask people what is stopping them from going after and achieving their dreams, I hear comments like: "I don't have the money." "I don't have the time." "I don't have the education." "I don't have the resources," etc. On the surface, these are difficult obstacles. They are road blocks. But, I believe that more often than not, they are excuses. An obstacle is defined as "anything that stands in the way." An excuse is defined as "to justify, to release from an obligation."

Are you in any way letting fear -- fear of failure or fear of success -- stop you?

You will most likely have lots of things that will stand in your way. However, people who get what they want find alternative routes. They don't let the obstacles become an excuse for not moving forward.

Anytime you are stuck, you need to ask yourself, "How badly do I want it? What other path can I take?" Be honest with yourself -- there are trade-offs. Since it is almost impossible to have it all, don't beat yourself up ... just decide. Do you want it enough to do whatever it takes, for as long as it takes, to achieve your goal?

For example, one of my staff members (newly married, new homeowner) wants a new kitchen. Money is the obstacle. She and her husband need $12,000. They currently have $3,000. They want it done in 18 months. They see no way to make it happen.

Is money an obstacle or an excuse? She and I sat down to analyze the obstacle. She needed $9,000 more; $9,000 divided by 18 months (completion date) means she needs to save $500 a month. When I asked her how they could put away $500 per month, she immediately said, "We can sell our 3rd car which we don't need, eat out less, bring lunch to work, use gift money and limit vacations." Then she said, "We can do it! I never thought we could. It seemed so overwhelming."

Regardless of your goal, whether it's saving money, getting an education, getting into shape, or writing a book, take a look at your obstacles. Then start figuring out how to minimize or eliminate them.

You have already picked your five top dreams and turned them into goals by adding completion dates.

Now go back to that list and select one.

Goal

_____

_____

Now, write down all of the obstacles that you could possibly face in achieving this goal.

Obstacles:

1.
2.
3.
4.
5.
6.
7.
8.
9.
10.

Go through each obstacle and brainstorm how you can overcome it. Also, be honest with yourself. Are these real obstacles, or are you using them as excuses?

Partners
Review the obstacle list with each other. Help each other by brainstorming ways to overcome the obstacles. Discuss way to discard the excuses and think of solutions to the "real" obstacles.

Olympic Obstacles - Aelin Peterson

Aelin Peterson never could have imagined that she'd be racing down a snow-covered mountain, risking bodily injury during the 2002 Winter Olympics as a member of the U.S. Cross-Country ski team -- not when she was a stock trader making $65,000 a year in a secure desk job.

You see, she had started out as a teenage skiing sensation and went on to compete in the World University Games. At age 20, however, a bout with viral meningitis and burnout took its toll -- dimming the light on her skiing brilliance.

Peterson shifted gears and took an internship at the investment bank Brown Brothers Harriman & Co. Before she was hired full time there, the skiing bug bit again -- so Peterson decided to shift her focus. This time she pursued Olympic speed skating.

Without a job, car, or anywhere to sleep, she moved to Milwaukee to train. Peterson took a job at Strong Capital Management to help support herself. While her competitive speed skating dreams didn't turn into reality, she soon climbed the corporate ladder and became a junior trader. After three years of success and glory as a trader, Peterson again felt the call of competitive winter sports. She felt unhealthy and that her body needed to race again -- thus the journey back to her love of skiing.

So, she moved to Alaska, entered a race and finished last. But Peterson didn't give up -- far from it. She wiped out her savings and kept on going. At the end of January 2002's national championships, she was the 4th-ranked female skier in America, and earned a spot on the U.S. Olympic cross-country ski team.

"How many working women are able to take a risk like this?" Peterson said in *BusinessWeek*. "I know I've been given a luxury. But if other working women have some unfulfilled goals that have been sadly tucked away, I would like to think that they would see me and take a shot at their own dreams."

No amount of obstacles, health, money or successes stopped Aelin Peterson. She was willing to sacrifice her security to go after her dream.

"Great works are performed not by strength, but by perseverance."

-- Dr. Samuel Johnson

"You will never possess what you are unwilling to pursue."

-- Dr. Alan Zimmerman

Chapter 4

Create Your Dream Team

"I get by with a little help from my friends."

-- The Beatles

"Keep away from people who try to belittle your ambitions. Small people always do that, but the really great make you feel that you, too, can become great."

-- Mark Twain

My parents were from the "do-it-yourself school." In our house, it was a sign of weakness to ask for help. I thought that was the way everyone operated. When I look back at the hours, even years, wasted trying to find things, do things, write things, etc., I realize now it would have been much easier to get the help I needed.

I learned a great lesson from a friend. After struggling with a project for a month, I mentioned it to a fellow speaker who said, "Why didn't you call me? I could have given you that information immediately." I said, "I didn't want to bother you." He then said, "How would you feel if I had asked you for help?" I responded, "I would have been flattered." He said, "Why don't you give others the same pleasure?"

Wow! What a wake-up call.

I'm not suggesting that you ask others to do the work for you, but I do think they may have resources, information, ideas, and maybe even a helping hand available. Why do you have to go after your dream alone?

Of course, you do have to ask the right people. People who want you to succeed, people who will boost your spirits when necessary, people who believe in you and people who are resources. A word of caution … avoid at all cost any negative people. They will drag you down with their negativity and narrow thinking. It is often difficult to avoid them, but if you truly want to pursue your dreams, you must stay away from them, or minimize their impact on you.

My dad was normally very supportive of what I chose to do. (Maybe it was because I typically chose what he wanted.) When I was deciding whether or not to take an early retirement from my 22-year career as a college professor to pursue my dream of being a full-time speaker and coach, I asked my dad for his opinion. His response, "Are you crazy! You have two children to support."

His negativity was fear. Fear for my children and me. How could I leave a tenured position with benefits to do something that was so risky? Then I realized that he had spent his whole life in a family business even though he was miserable. He always had an excuse as to why he stayed.

Fortunately for me, I had positive people in my life. My fiance Alan said, "What do you have to lose?" I said, "I could fail." He then said, "And then what?" He knew that I could create options for my children and myself. He didn't want fear to get in my way. I also got encouragement from my two daughters. "Mom," they said, "We trust you will always be able to take care of us. You should go after your dream."

Sometimes people can see things in you that you don't ever see yourself.

"Your choice of people to associate with, both personally and business-wise, is one of the most important choices you make. If you associate with turkeys, you will never fly with the eagles."

-- Brian Tracy

Now it's your turn:

Think back to a time when you had the support of family, friends, colleagues or paid professionals who helped you achieve your goals. Record the details.

_____
_____
_____
_____
_____
_____
_____
_____
_____
_____
_____

What did you learn from this?

_____
_____
_____
_____
_____
_____
_____
_____

Partners
Share the experience with your partner.

Who do you want on your dream team? Who will be able to provide ideas, information, encouragement, and other needed resources for you? List the people:

_____

_____

_____

_____

_____

_____

_____

_____

_____

Write specific resources that you will need:

_____

_____

_____

_____

_____

_____

_____

_____

_____

_____

_____

_____

_____

_____

Partners
Discuss with partner.

_____

Sarah Hughes

Most 6-year-old girls probably dream of Barbies and other childhood pursuits.

Not Sarah Hughes. When she was this tender age, Hughes dreamt of wearing an Olympic figure skating gold medal.

During the 2002 Olympic Winter Games, Hughes' childhood dream turned into reality. Despite being the underdog and unknown entity on the more experienced (and awarded) U.S. women's figure skating team of Michele Kwan and Sasha Cohen, this 16-year-old showed amazing poise, grace and skill on the ice.

The end result? Ten years after she dreamt of Olympic gold, Hughes was on the top tier of the award platform hearing her national anthem played.

Sarah Hughes couldn't have accomplished goals without the help she received from her parents and her coach. This team and her own passion, persistence and patience led her to victory.

"You can get everything in life you want if you will just help enough other people get what they want."

-- Zig Ziglar

Chapter 5

If It's Meant to Be ... It's Up to Me

"I think I can, I think I can, I think I can."

-- The Little Engine That Could

"Success: Willing to do what the average person is not willing to do."

-- Anonymous

"Let me tell you the secret that has led me to my goal. My strength lies solely in my tenacity."

-- Louis Pasteur

Remember your past successes? Remember all of your strengths? You will need all of that as you lead your dream team. You are the leader -- it is your dream. Don't let self doubt creep into the picture. The minute you start thinking negative thoughts, the chances of being successful diminish.

Thomas Edison said, "If we all did what we were capable of doing, we would literally astonish ourselves."

Think about the times you surprised yourself with what you were able to accomplish.

Write your overall qualities that have helped you in the past.

_____

_____

_____

_____

_____

_____

_____

_____

_____

_____

_____

_____

_____

_____

_____

_____

_____

_____

Partners
Share with each other.

If It's Meant to Be ... It's Up to Me

What specific strengths and qualities do you have that will help you achieve this dream?

_____

_____

_____

_____

_____

_____

_____

_____

_____

_____

_____

_____

_____

_____

_____

_____

_____

Write a positive self affirmation. Example: I think I can, I think I can ...

_____

_____

_____

_____

_____

_____

_____

_____

"My success is due more to vision than sight. I remember, as if it were yesterday, the devastation I felt the morning I woke up and realized I was blind. I instantly knew that all of my previous goals of being an NFL football player were gone. I had to either find new goals or give up on life. Since then, I have been a National Champion Olympic weightlifter, a successful owner of an Emmy award-winning television network, the author of a dozen books and a highly sought-after platform speaker."

"None of these things would have been possible in my old, sighted world, not because I lacked the talent but because I lacked the vision. People in our society spend far too much time worrying about how others see them and far too little time concerned with how they see themselves."

-- Jim Stovall

"I don't dream at night, I dream all day; I dream for a living."

-- Steven Spielberg

Chapter 6

Make it Happen

"Success doesn't come to you ... you go to it."

-- Marva Collins

"Goals are the maps to your dreams. If you don't have goals providing the direction, how will you find your way there? If you have a plan, and if you have your direction laid out, you can chart your progress to your dreams at each step along the way."

-- Mike Shanahan

Now it is time to create a plan to make the goal become a reality. You need to break down the steps that are necessary into small, manageable pieces. Each step will include a targeted date and list the necessary people and/or resources that will help you complete that step. Of course, record when you have completed it so you can move to the next action step.

Be realistic when you add a date. Be realistic when you look at necessary resources. Being realistic will help you get results and not get discouraged. I wish you much success turning your dreams into reality.

After college, my daughter, Julie, moved to San Francisco to "find her passion." She always had an interest in the environment, but managed to avoid all science courses in college except "Physics for Poets." While waiting on tables, she explored areas of interest. In time she decided she wanted to study Urban Forestry and become a certified arborist.

I sent her back to do her homework. She needed to figure out what it would require.

She called to tell me that it would require two years of undergraduate science courses (all the ones she avoided in college) to get into a master's program, complete her master's degree then field work while getting certified.

As she spoke, the enormity of the goal began to register. I heard, "What if I don't like the courses, what if I don't do well? What if I change my mind, what if I'm 30 by the time I am done?" After all of the "what if's" she said, "I might as well give up."

She was looking at possible roadblocks and was becoming overwhelmed. This is often a typical response, which is why so many people quit.

My advice to her was to take one course and see if she liked it. See how she does with it and then decide if she wants to take the next. In other words, *it's like eating an elephant. You need to do it one bite at a time.*

I also reminded her that in five years she would be 30 with or without achieving her dream. Never let time or age deter you from going after what you want.

Julie's action plan looked like this: ⟶

Goal -- Become a Certified Arborist: 2003

Action steps	Target date	Team/resources	Completed
Take 2 years of undergraduate science courses	1998	$$ -waiting tables	X
Apply to UC Davis - get accepted	2000	Advisor	X
Attend UC Davis	Fall 2000	Grant money	X
Complete course work	Spring 2002	Advisor Grant money	X
Write thesis	Winter 2003	Advisor - Mentor	X
Defend thesis	Winter 2003		X
Apply for job	Winter 2003	Wait tables for $	X
Get a job	Spring/Summer 2003	Web, network, newspapers, advisor	
Take certification course	Summer 2003		
Take exam	By end of 2003		

Affirmations:

"I have what it takes and will do what it takes to become a certified arborist."

"I will become a certified arborist."

As you work your plan, you might have to alter the dates, and add (or delete) members of your dream team. Yet if you want it badly enough (passion, persistence, patience), you will ultimately achieve it.

Once you have written your plan, post it so that you can reference it regularly. Now it's time for you to create your own action plan.

"The secret of success is constancy to purpose."

-- Benjamin Disraeli

"If I had to select one quality, one personal characteristic that I regard as being most highly correlated with success, whatever the field, I would pick the trait of persistence. Determination. The will to endure to the end, to get knocked down seventy times and get up off the floor saying, 'Here comes number seventy-one!'"

-- Richard M. Devos

"Act as though it is impossible to fail."

-- Anonymous

Goal _____

Action steps	**Target date**	**Team/resources**	**Completed**
1			
2			
3			
4			
5			
6			
7			
8			
9			
10			

Affirmations:

"Act as though it is impossible to fail."

-- Anonymous

Goal _____

Action steps	Target date	Team/resources	Completed
1			
2			
3			
4			
5			
6			
7			
8			
9			
10			

Affirmations:

"Act as though it is impossible to fail."

-- Anonymous

Goal _____

Action steps	**Target date**	**Team/resources**	**Completed**
1			
2			
3			
4			
5			
6			
7			
8			
9			
10			

Affirmations:

"Act as though it is impossible to fail."

-- Anonymous

Goal _____

Action steps	Target date	Team/resources	Completed
1			
2			
3			
4			
5			
6			
7			
8			
9			
10			

Affirmations:

"Act as though it is impossible to fail."

-- Anonymous

Goal _____

Action steps	**Target date**	**Team/resources**	**Completed**
1			
2			
3			
4			
5			
6			
7			
8			
9			
10			

Affirmations:

""Act as though it is impossible to fail."

-- Anonymous

Goal _____

Action steps	**Target date**	**Team/resources**	**Completed**
1			
2			
3			
4			
5			
6			
7			
8			
9			
10			

Affirmations:

"Act as though it is impossible to fail."

-- Anonymous

Goal _____

Action steps	Target date	Team/resources	Completed
1			
2			
3			
4			
5			
6			
7			
8			
9			
10			

Affirmations:

"Act as though it is impossible to fail."

-- Anonymous

Goal _____

Action steps	**Target date**	**Team/resources**	**Completed**
1			
2			
3			
4			
5			
6			
7			
8			
9			
10			

Affirmations:

"Act as though it is impossible to fail."

-- Anonymous

Goal _____

Action steps	Target date	Team/resources	Completed
1			
2			
3			
4			
5			
6			
7			
8			
9			
10			

Affirmations:

Chapter 7

More Inspiration

"At first, our dreams seem impossible, then improbable and eventually, inevitable."

-- Christopher Reeve

For inspiration, **the following quotes and stories may be helpful:**

"It's no use saying you are doing your best. You have to do what is necessary."

-- Winston Churchill

"Unless you're willing to have a go, fail miserably and have another go, success won't happen."

-- Philip Adams

"Success is simply a matter of luck. Ask any failure."

-- Earl Nightingale

"Choice, not circumstances, determines your success."

-- Anonymous

"Success seems to be connected with action. Successful men keep moving. They make mistakes, but they don't quit."

-- Conrad Hilton

"Desire is the way to motivation, but it's the determination and commitment to an unrelenting pursuit of your goal -- a commitment to excellence -- that will enable you to attain the success you seek."

-- Mario Andretti

Heather Rafferty

Career Change Can be Good: Balancing Work/Personal Life

Having a high power position in Manhattan just didn't cut it for Heather Rafferty. She was fast approaching career burnout and missing out on some of life's many opportunities.

While she still works 50 hours a week at her current job — Communications Manager at The Culinary Institute of America in Hyde Park, New York — Rafferty now has more time to devote to personal interests.

In an article that appeared in *Shape* magazine, Rafferty explained, "I threw in the towel and revamped my entire life. Now I have time to reconnect with the people who are important in my life, and to nurture the relationships with my friends that I had tossed aside for a few years, as well as to pursue my hobbies."

Once Rafferty decided her goal was to have more free time to devote to personal endeavors, she faced several obstacles. She said, "The primary obstacle was fear of the unknown because it often paralyzed me into inaction. I wondered, 'What would happen if this didn't work out? How hard would it be to move to a new place where I knew no one? What if I hated my new job? What if my then partner (now husband) couldn't make the move with me?'"

Rafferty received help from her family and spouse to overcome this obstacle and achieve her goal. "I had a lot of support from my husband and parents. They encouraged me whenever I began to doubt myself," she explained.

"I now feel like a different person. I have a whole new perspective now."

Despite the obstacles, Rafferty was able to push forward. Her passion and persistence paid off!

Kristen and Todd Stein

Kristen and Todd had a goal -- a goal many people have — to be parents. But for them it wasn't an easy path. After trying to conceive for several years, they went to a fertility doctor who did the standard testing. They could find nothing wrong. They kept trying and the clock kept ticking. After years, they decided to adopt. Their first choice was to adopt a baby from the U.S. They wanted a healthy Caucasian infant. They contacted adoption agencies -- but were told that they were too old. They contacted lawyers who kept coming up with nothing. The clock kept ticking.

Finally, they found a young woman who was committed to giving up her baby. For 8 months, Kristen and Todd were in constant contact with the young woman. They gave financial and emotional support. Plans were made for Kristen and Todd to be at the delivery. They painted the baby's room in their home, bought the layette, and had a local pediatrician scheduled. At the beginning of the ninth month, the birth mother received a call from the child's father. Although he had not been in contact with her since she told him that she was pregnant, he decided that he wanted the baby despite her wishes.

Even if he ultimately changed his mind, it was too risky for Kristen and Todd to bring the baby home and then lose it to the father.

Despair! Todd was willing to stop. He couldn't stand to see the heartache that Kristen went through with each disappointment. And they weren't getting any younger.

Kristen was not ready or willing to give up. She figured there had to be another way to fulfill her dream of becoming a mother.

They decided that China was the answer. Initially, they wanted a healthy Caucasian infant, but that no longer seemed as important. They knew they could love a child that didn't look like them. After a long process they went to China and came home with 17-month-old Lexie.

Lexie Stein, now 3, is a well-adjusted American child. Her parents say that their persistence and patience paid off. They are so happy and so proud. Ultimately, everything worked out for the very best.

Nothing was going to deter them from having a child. When one method of getting a child shut down, they explored others until they found one that worked. Even though the process took many years ... it was well worth the wait.

Martha J. Williams

You might think a business owner that went through four business partners and two bankruptcy proceedings would say, "Enough!" ... but not Martha J. Williams.

No, this entrepreneur never stopped dreaming and turning those dreams into realities — despite encountering many obstacles along the way.

Martha Williams was the first African American woman in the United States to own a plastic injection molding facility, and her success has not come easy. Her firm, StyleMaster Inc., was born in 1991 after she was able to obtain the necessary funding from traditional and other sources. A few design successes later, and Williams was on her way.

According to an article in *Minority Business Entrepreneur* (MBE) magazine, Williams says the support of her long-time companion, Clarence Jefferson, made it possible for her to build the business and have a fulfilling family life. This support also helped Williams make it through two Chapter 11 bankruptcy proceedings as well as disputes with many former partners/investors.

Williams attributes her "never give up" business outlook to many factors, including her mother. She says she is also a true self-motivator who lives her life from goal to goal.

"Failure is not in my vocabulary," Williams said in the MBE article. "I can't fail. It's just not acceptable. I've had people ask me if [the financial problems/bankruptcies] weren't failures, and the answer is absolutely not. I've never stopped. There are stumbling blocks, but as long as you don't give up, that's what's important. You have to find a way to get through the brick wall or over the mountain. You just have to."

Jim and Sandy

Jim and Sandy were very lucky, at least according to their friends and family. But on this particular Sunday afternoon as they packed their suitcases and their briefcases and prepared for yet another week of travel, away from one another, away from their home — feeling "lucky" was the furthest thing from their minds.

Yes, they had secure jobs in industries that were doing well and their incomes were more than they had imagined and more than their parents had ever had. It wasn't that they hated their jobs or their companies. It was more that they saw life passing them by.

They were both about to turn 40, and the children they had long imagined having were not yet a reality. Their greatest joy came from the moments they shared with their two dogs, Grace and Simon. It was during those times, as a family of two loyal canines and two adoring humans, that life was simple and rich and full of promise.

Adding to their heavy mood was the recent death of Sandy's dad, her greatest supporter and inspiration. Jim, too, had been deeply touched by the love of this man and moved by how fully he had lived life. What would he have to say about the choices they were making?

That Sunday afternoon became a turning point for Jim and Sandy. They stopped numbly placing their clothes and toiletries into their bags and decided to talk, to really talk about how they wanted to live the rest of their lives. They talked about what was important to them and what was not. They shared their fears and their dreams. They surprised each other with how much they had harbored the same doubts and the same longings.

And then, they did something they had never done before. Instead of swallowing all of their emotions with a wistful sigh and going right back to what they had been doing, they took out blank sheets of paper. They began to create a plan, a plan that would give them a life of nights and weekends together, a life with the children they longed for, and a life that they wouldn't wish away with thoughts of "someday."

Hours later they looked at each other with hope and excitement. They had a magnificent plan! Over the course of the next three years they would systematically move away from their corporate worlds. Jim would transition first, because his computer skills would allow independent consulting from home. Sandy would follow after certain financial goals were attained.

Their plan was to turn their love of animals into their own business where they would board, groom and train dogs. They would start by attending conferences for people who were interested in this business, by researching demand for these services (something they knew existed from personal experience) and by finding a piece of property with lots of land and a place where they could have both a home and a kennel.

They mapped out timelines and identified people in their life who they knew would offer love, support and encouragement. They made a promise to share their dream and plan with only those who made that list. They became singularly focused on this shared goal. Their weekends were now full of purpose.

Spending was no longer all about impulse purchases to try to fill the void they used to feel. Their universe expanded to include volunteer work on Saturdays with an organization that trained assistance dogs for disabled individuals. Their family of two dogs grew to four. They were laughing more and sighing less.

Within one year from that memorable Sunday afternoon, they purchased a house with 23 acres. It was old and small and needed lots of work. Jim was now working from home and had created flexibility in his schedule that allowed him to spend time renovating the house.

Today, three years later, Sandy and Jim live with their four dogs in that beautiful home. There are fields, woods, babbling brooks and a magnificent second building that will soon be a vacation getaway for the dogs of countless people who are already making reservations for their beloved pets.

Sandy and Jim are in the process of adopting their first child and no longer spend Sunday afternoons organizing their travel agendas and packing suits.

Now it is *your* turn to follow your dreams! Use this guidebook to help you along your journey. I wish you much luck and would love to hear from you. If you need help with your action plan or if you would like to share your success stories — please e-mail me at: mbrody@BrodyCommunications.com.

Keep dreaming! Keep doing what you have to do to turn your dreams into reality!

Appendix

About Brody Communications Ltd.

How We Can Help You ...

Brody Communications Ltd. is an international business skills company that provides customized training programs and one-on-one coaching in the areas of communication and presentation skills, and management/leadership development. Since 1983, our team of agile, dedicated professionals has been committed to helping individuals and organizations succeed. Contact us to see how we can help you: 800-726-7936; sign up for our free quarterly newsletter at www.BrodyCommunications.com

Learning Tools: Career Skills Press, a division of Brody Communications Ltd., offers a wide range of books, audio and videotapes, E-books and a CD-ROM. Check out our shopping cart for more information at www.BrodyCommunications.com.

Marjorie Brody can speak at your upcoming meeting: Her energetic message, interactive methods and proven strategies help people get what they want and advance their careers -- in turn helping their companies to grow and profit. She also can become your success partner as an **executive coach**.

For more information on booking Marjorie as a speaker or executive coach, visit www.MarjorieBrody.com or call 800-726-7936.